IELTS Writing Academic Test

Model reports and how to write them!

About the author

I have been teaching English as a second language for over fifteen years in Taiwan and Australia, in language centres and universities. I have also been working as an IELTS examiner. My area of specialization is teaching students how to pass the IELTS exam. I particularly enjoy teaching IELTS because I find it challenging to teach students the necessary skills and strategies that they need to pass, and I also find that my students are highly motivated – this is a joy for a teacher!

Other books in this series

Answers for IELTS Letter Writing
Answers for IELTS Essay Writing

Acknowledgements

I would like to thank those responsible for their help in completing this book. I sincerely thank Phil Biggerton for his time editing this book, and for me to use tasks from his book: IELTS - The Complete Guide to Task 1 Writing. I would also like to thank some of my faithful students, Nhi Phan, Andrey Polyakov, and Maria Gvozdeva, for providing valuable feedback on this book. Thanks to all my past students as well, for giving me the inspiration and desire to write this book.

Copyright

Contents

1. Overview

Writing Task 1 is designed to test your ability to explain information shown in a **process diagram, flow chart, line graph, bar graph, pie chart, table, map, or floor plan.** You must present the information in your own words as complete sentences within paragraphs. You are required to write over 150 words, and the task should be completed in 20 minutes (both part 1 and 2 must be finished in 1 hour). You are not asked to give opinions, make assumptions, or draw conclusions about the information given. Note that most of the parts of the task are standardised. For instance, you are always advised to spend about 20 minutes on the task and write at least 150 words. In addition you are always advised to *summarise the information by selecting and reporting the main features*.

Sample question: WRITING TASK 1

You should spend about 20 minutes on this task.

> **The graph below shows information about the activities that New Zealand and Australian children enjoy doing the most in 2007.**
>
> Summarise the information by selecting and reporting the main features, and make comparisons where relevant.

Write at least 150 words.

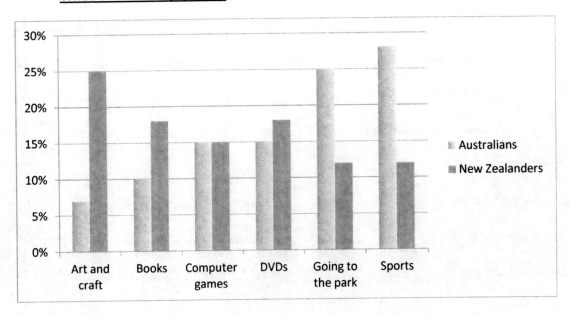

What Children enjoy doing

1.1. Grading of tasks

Criteria	Requirement
Task Achievement	✓ write over 150 words ✓ satisfy all the requirements of the task ✓ introduce the task (rephrase the question) ✓ give a summary of the key features ✓ highlight key features
Coherence and Cohesion	✓ sequence information and ideas logically ✓ use paragraphing appropriately ✓ make sure there is a clear progression throughout ✓ use a range of cohesive devices appropriately ✓ avoid unnecessary repetition of information
Lexical Resource	✓ rephrase vocabulary to show your range of vocabulary ✓ use adverbs and adjectives to show precision ✓ use less common lexical items ✓ awareness of style and collocation ✓ avoid errors with word formation ✓ avoid errors with spelling ✓ avoid errors with word choices
Grammatical Range and Accuracy	✓ use a mix of simple and complex sentence forms ✓ produce error-free sentences ✓ avoid errors with grammar and punctuation

Tip!
You will only achieve a high overall score by focusing on all four criteria for the writing exam.

Copyright: www.ieltsanswers.com Mike Wattie 2012   5

1.2.   Types of tasks

Task one of the IELTS writing exam includes different types of tasks. The most common ones are: tables, pie charts, bar charts, line graphs, process diagrams, flow charts, maps and floor plans, which should all be looked at to be well prepared. Then, task one of the IELTS writing exam can be separated into two key types. Static tasks, which are tasks that have only one time period; and change over time tasks, which have two or more different time periods. Finally, with task one of the IELTS writing exam, you need to use different types of language depending on whether the task consists of numbers, percentages, or steps in a process. Therefore, there are three key dimensions of task one of the IELTS writing exam:

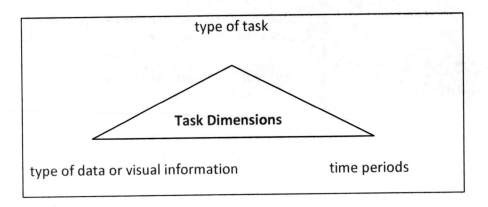

Tip!
Before you start writing, make sure you are very clear about the type of task, whether the task is about numbers or percentages, and whether the task involves a single time period or many.

The names of different types of tasks

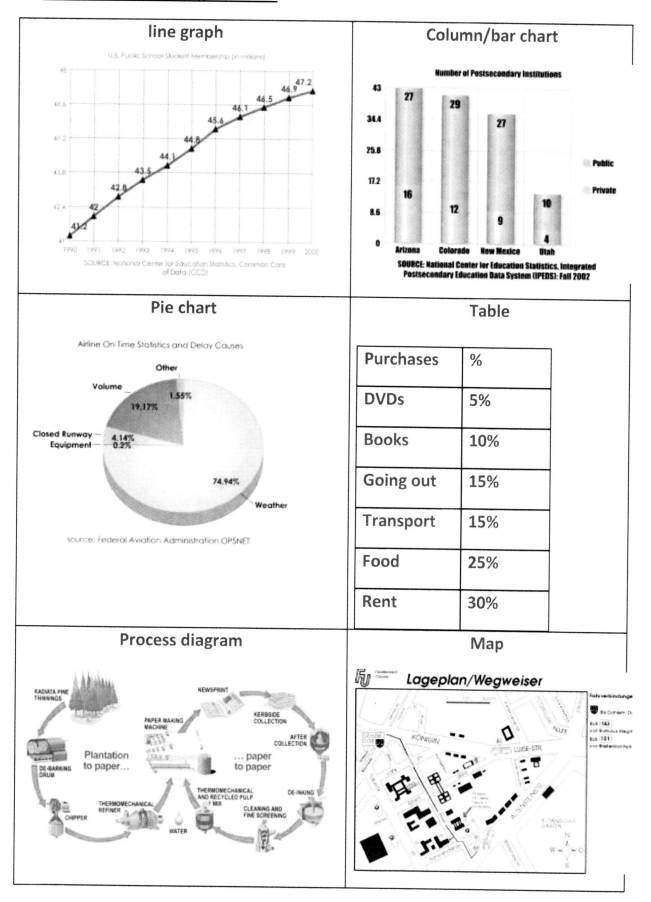

How to Improve

1. Learn how the test is structured and graded

2. Learn skills and language to improve your answers

3. Practice using the skills and language

4. Write lots of tasks. If you want to have your essay assessed by an experienced examiner and tutor visit this page: http://www.ieltsanswers.com/IELTS-Writing-Correction.html

Task Sequence for Writing: Academic Task 1:

You have about 20 minutes to complete this task. I recommend you spend your time as follows:

1. Spend about 2 to 3 minutes analysing and planning the task

2. Spend about 14 to 15 minutes writing it

3. If you have time, spend a couple of minutes to check what you have written.

> *Tip!*
> **Before you go to your exam you should have a clear idea of the steps you will follow to write your report.**

A step-by-step approach

1. Read the Task.

2. Paraphrase keywords in the task instructions.

3. Work out what information is given and what type of task it is.

4. Decide if this is a static (same time period) or change over time task.

5. Be clear about whether the data is about percentages or numbers.

4. Identify the highlights of the task. There should be about ten critical points that should be mentioned for each task.

5. Work out the overall summary. There should be one or two key points that must be mentioned for each task.

6. Plan the structure of the answer. Always look for ways the data can be logically grouped into paragraphs.

7. Write your answer.

8. Proofread your answer if time permits.

1.3.   Planning

It is essential that you make a solid plan before you start writing your report. This will make sure that you cover all the key data, which helps you maximise your score for task achievement. In addition, it will help you to organise your data logically, which will increase your score for cohesion and coherence. Overall, you should spend about two or 3 minutes making a plan. A few key aspects of this process are explained below.

Selecting data to include

When writing your report you are supposed to highlight the key data and not just list the data. The Golden Rule to remember is that as the amount of data increases you must be more selective when selecting it. You need about ten key points.

Tip!
Making a plan saves you time when you write your report and ensures you cover all the key points using an appropriate structure.

Static tasks

Usually with tasks that have a single time period (static tasks) you want to focus on numbers that are the highest, lowest, or the same. The key data is circled in the table below to illustrate this.

	USA	Uk	Canada	Australia	France	Egypt
Beef	220 a	240 c	160 e	200	150	120
Lamb	150	170	160	130	50 h	60
Chicken	120	120 d	160 f	50 g	40	20 i
Pork	100 b	230	450	450	450	200 j

a. In the USA beef sales were <u>the highest</u> at 220 grams.

b. In the United States pork sales were <u>the lowest</u> at only 100.

c. In the UK beef sales were <u>the most</u> at 240.

d. In the United Kingdom chicken sales were <u>the least</u> at 120

e. In Canada the sales of beef Lamb and chicken <u>were all the same</u>.

f. The volume of pork sold in Canada, Australia and France <u>were identical</u>.

g. Chicken was <u>the lowest selling meat</u> in Australia

h. Lamb and chicken <u>sold the least,</u> in France, at only about 50 grams.

i. <u>The least popular meat</u> was chicken at 20 grams in Egypt.

j. <u>In Egypt the most popular meat</u> was pork at 200 grams.

Note: you should connect some of these items together in sentences, so if we look at items "i" and "j" we could write: In Egypt, <u>the least popular meat</u> was chicken at 20 grams, and <u>the most popular meat</u> was pork at 200 grams.

Change over time tasks

Usually with tasks that have multiple time periods (change over time tasks) you want to focus on beginning numbers, peaks and low points, categories that overtake another category, and ending numbers. The key data is shown in the line chart below to illustrate this.

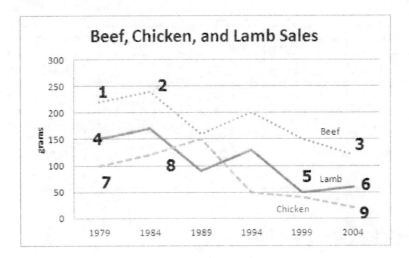

1. In 1979 about 220 grams of beef <u>were</u> sold.

2. The purchasing of beef <u>peaked at</u> less than 250 grams in 1984.

3. In 2004, beef consumption <u>fell to</u> around 120 grams.

4. At the beginning of the period lamb sales <u>stood at</u> 150 grams.

5. The amount of lamb sold <u>reached a low point of</u> 50 grams in 1999.

6. At the end of the period lamb sales <u>were approximately</u> 60 grams.

7. Chicken sales <u>started off at</u> 100 grams.

8. Sales of chicken increased rapidly, and around 1985 they <u>rose to over</u> 130 grams <u>overtaking</u> the sales of lamb.

9. By the end of the period chicken sales <u>had fallen to their lowest point</u> at about 25 grams.

Combining data

Combining data of two or more categories is a way to reduce the total number of words you need to write to make sure you can write a good task response in about 20 or so minutes you have to write your report. In addition, it is a good way to write more complex sentences to increase your score for grammar. Below is an example of how you can combine data. The word respectively is a useful word.

An example:

Beef and lamb showed a similar significant downward trend throughout the period. Beef and lamb started at 220 and 150 grams, respectively; and by the end of the period they plunged to approximately 120 and 60 grams, respectively. Beef sales peaked at about 240 grams in 1984. Lamb reached a low point of about 50 grams in 1999.

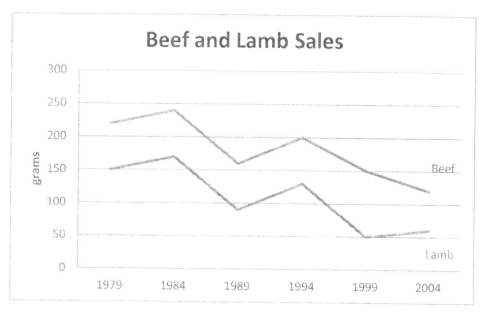

> *Tip!*
> **Combining data is especially useful; when you are given a lot of data to enable you to complete the task on time.**

1.4.   *Grading of tasks*

Criteria	Requirement
Task Achievement	✓ write over 150 words ✓ satisfy all the requirements of the task ✓ introduce the task (rephrase the question) ✓ give a summary of the key features ✓ highlight key features
Coherence and Cohesion	✓ sequence information and ideas logically ✓ use paragraphing appropriately ✓ make sure there is a clear progression throughout ✓ use a range of cohesive devices appropriately ✓ avoid unnecessary repetition of information
Lexical Resource	✓ rephrase vocabulary to show your range of vocabulary ✓ use adverbs and adjectives to show precision ✓ use less common lexical items ✓ awareness of style and collocation ✓ avoid errors with word formation ✓ avoid errors with spelling ✓ avoid errors with word choices
Grammatical Range and Accuracy	✓ use a mix of simple and complex sentence forms ✓ produce error-free sentences ✓ avoid errors with grammar and punctuation

2.

> *Tip!*
> **You will only achieve a high overall score by focusing on all four criteria for the writing**

Single time (static) task

Task Instructions

The IELTS static task is designed to test your ability to compare and contrast information shown in a **line graph, bar graph, pie chart, table, process diagram, or map** (the last two tasks will be covered in a separate section). You must present the information in your own words as complete sentences within paragraphs. You are required to write over 150 words, and the task should be completed in 20 minutes (both part 1 and 2 must be finished in 1 hour).

Requires

1   Past or present tense

2   Comparison vocabulary to describe differences and similarities of data

How to Improve

1   Do exercises to improve comparatives and superlatives for comparing data

2   Do exercises to use the correct language with numbers and percentages

3   Read sample questions and answers

4   Learn how to correctly structure a static task

Useful language

Adjectives: Comparing and contrasting

A static task requires you to compare and contrast information, in order to achieve this it's important to use comparatives and superlatives. The following provides guidelines on how to form comparatives and superlatives.

All one syllable words and most two syllable words that end in "y" add *er* and *est*. All other two syllables or more words need to use *more* and *most*. Refer to the chart below.

One syllable	comparative	superlative
cheap	cheaper	cheapest
large	larger	largest

Two syllables "y"	comparative	superlative
happy	happier	happiest
lucky	luckier	luckiest

Two syllables	comparative	superlative
common	more common	most common
modern	more modern	most modern

Note: There are also some exceptions, such as the ones below:

good   better best

bad   worse worst

Complete the table with the correct comparative and superlative forms [answers are at the back of this book]

word	comparative	superlative
1. accurate	*more accurate*	*most accurate*
2. certain		
3. pretty		
4. cool		
5. correct		
6. dangerous		
7. easy		
8. modern		
9. funny		
10. new		
11. possible		
12. probable		
13. up-to-date		

Tip!
Use comparatives and superlatives to compare data and increase your score for task achievement. It also helps increase your score for vocabulary.

Language with numbers and percentages

When writing your report you must carefully identify whether the information that is given involves countable data (trees), uncountable data (water), or percentages (15%). This is because the language used with the three types is different. If you use the incorrect language the examiner will easily identify it and your vocabulary score will be lowered.

Countable numbers

The <u>number</u> of trees was 100.

The <u>quantity</u> of trees was 100.

Uncountable numbers

The <u>amount</u> of water used was 100 litres.

Percentages

The <u>rate</u> of water usage was 15 <u>per cent</u>.

The <u>proportion of</u> water usage was <u>15%</u>

The water usage was <u>fifteen per cent.</u>

The water usage increased by <u>15 percent.</u>

The <u>percentages of</u> water usage <u>(15%)</u> and power usage <u>(16%)</u> were about the same.

The water usage and power usage were <u>15%</u> and <u>16%,</u> respectively.

Exercise 2: Language with numbers and percentages

Circle the correct word. The answers are at the back of this book.

1. The <u>number/amount</u> of cars was over 1,000.

2. The <u>rate/ number</u> of electricity usage was 15 per cent.

3. The <u>amount /percentage</u> of power was 15%.

4. The <u>number/amount</u> of trains was 100.

5. The <u>number /proportion</u> of lamb consumed increased by 15 percent.

6. The <u>percentage/amount</u> of lamb (15%) and chicken (16%) were about the same.

7. The <u>number/amount</u> of beer consumed was 100 litres.

8. The <u>proportion/ amount</u> of water usage and power usage were 15% and 16%, respectively.

9. The <u>number/percentage</u> of apples was 10 on Fridays.

10. The <u>number/amount</u> of oil produced was 100 litres.

2.1. Steps to complete a static task:

1. Read and underline key vocabulary in the question and write words with the same or related meaning.

2. Check whether the data is about percentages or numbers.

   For percentages use: proportion, %, per cent, rate, one-third, two-thirds.

   For numbers use: amount for uncountable nouns, number for countable nouns.

3. Brainstorm key points for the answer, look for the following:

   Striking numbers/percentages (highest and lowest)

   Comparisons (higher and lower data)

   Similarities (the same)

   Data that can be combined (similarities)

4. Identify the highlights of the task. There should be about 10 critical points that should be mentioned for each task. They should be identified in your brainstorming above.

5. Work out the overall summary. There should be one or two key points that must be mentioned.

6. Plan the structure of answer (how can the data be grouped).

7. Write the task.

8. Proofread the task.

2.2.   Sample static task

You should spend about 20 minutes on this task

The graph below shows information about the activities that Australian and New Zealand children enjoy doing the most in 2007.

Summarize the information by selecting and reporting the main features, and make comparisons where relevant.

Write at least 150 words

What Children enjoy doing

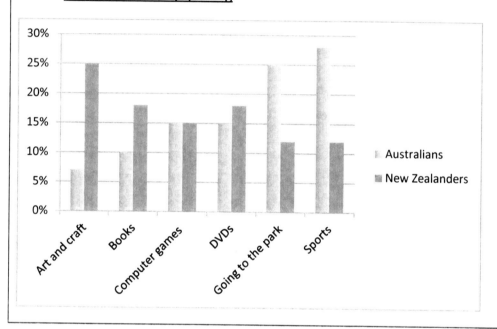

Model answer:

The bar graph illustrates data about the favourite recreational pursuits of children in two nations in 2007. Overall, Australians were more likely to do outdoor activities, whereas New Zealanders were more involved in indoor activities.

For Australian youths, the most popular activity was doing sporting activities, which accounted for approximately 28%. Next, a quarter of Australians enjoyed visiting parks. The third most popular leisure pursuits were video games and watching movies, which both attracted 15%. The least popular activities were reading, and art and craft, which accounted for about 10% and 7 %, respectively.

Turning to the young New Zealanders, the highest proportion of young people enjoyed doing art and craft, which accounted for 25% of them. This was followed by reading books and watching movies, which each accounted for roughly 17%. The proportion who played video games was only 15%. The least popular were trips to the park and playing sports at 13%.   [154 words]

> *Tip!*
> Note that the model answer above does not include a conclusion. You are not required to write a conclusion for a task 1 report.

Steps in planning the model task:

1. Read and underline key vocabulary in the question and write words with the same or related meaning.

The <u>graph</u> below <u>shows</u> <u>information</u> about the <u>activities</u> that <u>Australian</u> and <u>New Zealand</u>

bar graph   *illustrates*   *data*   *recreational pursuits* *Australians*   *New Zealanders*

children <u>enjoy doing the most</u> in 2007.

youths   *favourite*

2. Check whether the data is about percentages or numbers.

   percentages

3. Brainstorm key points for the answer, look for the following:

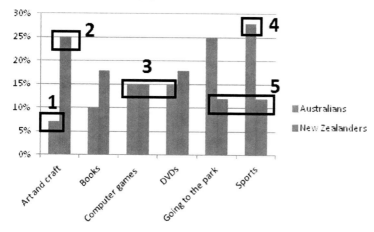

1 = lowest % for Australians

2= highest % for New Zealanders

3= same % for Australians AND same % for both nationalities for computer games

4= highest % for Australians

5=same % for New Zealanders

Below are some additional points worth mentioning.

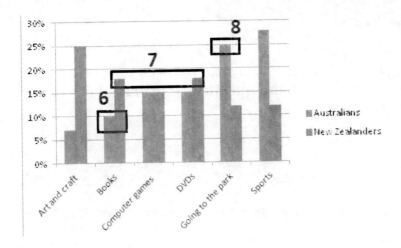

6= the second lowest % for Australians

7= the second to highest % for New Zealanders (for two categories)

8 = the second to highest % for Australians

4. Work out the overall summary. There should be one or two key points that must be mentioned.

For this task it could be the highest and lowest percentage for each country. But even more cleverly, it can be pointed out that Australians preferred outdoor activities and New Zealanders preferred indoor ones. This is because the top two percentages for Australians are both outdoor activities; and for New Zealanders the top two percentages are for indoor activities.

5. Plan the structure of the answer (how can the data be grouped).

Introduction = rephrase of the task introduction + overall summary

Australians = highest to lowest percentages

New Zealanders = highest to lowest percentages

6. Write the task.

The model answer is written above.

Double pie task

Often in the IELTS Task 1 academic exam you are given two pie charts. With two pie charts you can structure the body of your report either with a paragraph for each pie chart or by the categories of each pie. Each one has advantages. Structuring the essay with a paragraph about each pie chart is an easy structure, and you have two clear body paragraphs. You focus mostly on the highest and lowest figures of each pie chart and the comparison usually comes in the overall summary. It is also quicker to write.

Structuring the essay by categories of the chart allows for more comparisons to be made and can result in a better coverage of the data. It can be more difficult for the reader to see your structure if it is not written carefully. It can be harder to get logical body paragraphs and can just end in one big body paragraph. Getting logical separation of data has to be done on a case by case basis depending on the data of the particular task. For instance a paragraph could be written about the highest proportions and another one about the lowest proportions only if the highest and lowest proportions are the same in each pie graph.

I would pick ONE way, and always use this structure, so that you have it perfected before your exam. If your goal is 7 the safest way is by pie, but if you really want to get to 8 it could be worth the risk of going by category. Examples of both ways of writing the task are given below.

> **Tip!**
> **Develop habits for writing each type of task. These habits will help you speed up your writing, so you can finish on time in the exam.**

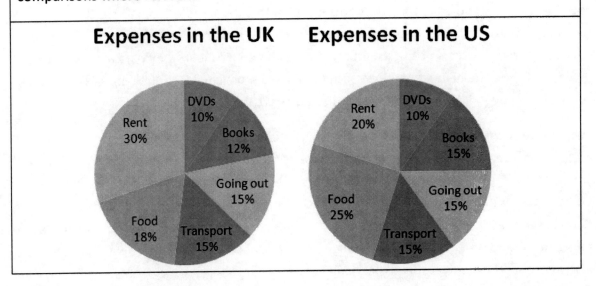

Model answer by category

[In the model report written below the structure is by category. One paragraph has the categories which have a different percentage in each country, and the other paragraph has the categories which are the same in both contracts.]

The pie charts compare weekly expenses of the six most common categories in America and United Kingdom. Overall, it is obvious from the charts that spending on rent accounted for the largest proportion in the UK, whilst in the United States it was food. In addition, expenditures on DVDs were the lowest in both of the nations.

It is clear from the pie charts that the proportion of expenditures varied for most categories. Rent accounted for a high proportion in both countries at 30% and 20% of the weekly spending in Great Britain and the USA, respectively. Americans spent a significantly higher proportion on food and books, which accounted for 25% and 15% of their weekly expenses, respectively. However, British spent only 18% and 12% on food and books.

Turning to items that both nations spent an equal proportion on, the expenditure for transportation, going out for entertainment, and on DVDs were the same proportion. People in both countries spent 15% of their weekly budget on transport and also on visiting places. The rate of spending on DVDs was slightly lower at 10%. [184 words]

Model answer by pie chart

[In the model answer below the structure is by pie charts. One paragraph describes the first pie chart and the second one describes the second pie chart.]

The pie charts compare weekly expenses of the six most common categories in America and United Kingdom. Overall, it is obvious from the charts that spending on rent accounted for the largest proportion in the UK, whilst in the United States it was food. In addition, expenditures on DVDs were the lowest in both of the nations.

In Britain the highest proportion was spent on accommodation, which accounted for 30%. Food was the second highest item of expense at 18%. The British spent exactly the same proportion on going out for entertainment and transportation [15%]. The lowest item of expenditure was DVDs at 10%.

Turning to America, groceries accounted for the highest proportion of expenditure at 25%. Transportation entertainment and reading materials each accounted for exactly fifteen per cent. As was the case in the UK, the lowest proportion was spent on DVDs, with the same percentage of 10%.

[151 words]

3. Change over time task

Task Instructions

The IELTS change over time task is designed to test your ability to explain information during different time periods shown in a **line graph, bar graph, pie chart, table, process diagram, or map** (the last two tasks will be covered in a separate section). You must present the information in your own words as complete sentences within paragraphs. You are required to write over 150 words, and the task should be completed in 20 minutes (both part 1 and 2 must be finished in 1 hour).

Requires

1 Past tense and sometimes future tense

2 Verb and noun phrases to describe trends

3 Verbs and nouns to describe data levels

4 Prepositions for time and data

How to Improve

1 Do exercises to improve the grammar and vocabulary to complete this kind of task

2 Read sample questions and answers

3 Learn how to correctly structure a change over time task

4 Practice writing *change over time* tasks

5 Receive feedback on practice tests

6 Use the feedback to improve your answers

Describing Trends:

↗	↘	—	/\/\/

Noun phrases			
an increase	a decrease	at a similar level	a fluctuation
a surge	a decline	a steady trend	an oscillation
a rise	a drop	maintained stability	
a jump	a tumble	a period of stability	
a leap	a plunge		

Verb phrases			
increased	decreased	stabilized	fluctuated
surged	declined	remained unchanged	oscillated
rose	plunged	remained static	
soared	tanked	stayed the same	
rocketed	sunk		

Describing specific points

a peak (noun) peaked (verb)	
a low point (noun) a nadir (noun)	
was overtaken by (verb) overtook (verb)	

Sentence structure

For a change over time task you should use the past tense and you should try to modify nouns with adjectives and verbs with adverbs to improve the precision of your task, which will improve your score for *task response* as well as for *vocabulary*.

Past tense:

      Was + adj + NOUN   VERB + adverb

Some illustrative examples

There was a slight INCREASE in the number of unemployed people.

The number of unemployed people INCREASED slightly.

There was a dramatic RISE in the amount of water.

The amount of water ROSE dramatically.

> **Tip!**
> **Modify your nouns and verbs with adjectives and adverbs in order to increase precision of describing data which increases your score for task achievement.**

Adjectives and adverbs according to the degree of change (biggest to smallest)

adjectives that modify the size	adjectives that modify the time
a dramatic...	a sudden...
a considerable...	a quick...
a steep	a rapid...
a sharp...	a steady...
a significant...	a gradual...
a substantial...	a slow...
a moderate...	
a slight...	

adverbs that modify the size	adverbs that modify the time
...dramatically	...suddenly
...considerably	...quickly
...steeply	...rapidly
...sharply	...steadily
...significantly	...gradually
...substantially	...slowly
...moderately	
...slightly	

Prepositions for time and data

Time

from 1900 to 2000

during the period from 1900 to 2000

from 1940 onwards

in 1940

Numbers

Use **amount** with things that cannot be counted but ' **number** ' with things that can be counted

The number of unemployed people increased from 1,000 to 2,000

The number of unemployed people increased by 1,000

reached a peak at 2,000

fell to its lowest point at 1,000

Tip!
Accuracy with prepositions is essential to reaching high scores for grammar.

Language with numbers and percentages

When writing your report you must carefully identify whether the information that is given involves countable data (trees), uncountable data (water), or percentages (15%). This is because the language used with the three types is different. If you use the incorrect language the examiner will easily identify it and your vocabulary score will be lowered. Use **number** with things that can be counted and **amount** with things that cannot be counted.

Countable numbers

The <u>number</u> of trees planted increased

Uncountable numbers

The <u>amount</u> of water used increased

Percentages

The <u>percentage</u> of water used increased by 15%.

The <u>proportion</u> of water used increased by 15%.

The <u>rate</u> of water usage increased by 15%.

The water usage increased by <u>15%</u>

The water usage increased by <u>15 per cent.</u>

The water usage increased by <u>15 percent.</u>

The water usage increased <u>(15%)</u>.

3.1. Steps to complete a change over time task

1. Read and underline key vocabulary in the question and try to rephrase them.

2. Check whether the data is about percentages or numbers.

- For percentages use: proportion, %, per cent, rate, one-third, two-thirds

- For numbers use: amount for uncountable nouns, number for countable nouns

3. Brainstorm key points for the answer, look for the following:

- beginning numbers

- ending numbers

- highest points

- lowest points

- data series that overtake other ones (e.g. line chart where one line crosses over another line)

- period of fluctuation, stability

- sudden changes of increase or decrease

4. Identify the highlights of the task. There should be about ten critical points that should be mentioned for each task. You must always cover all categories and all time periods, but you don't need to cover every category for every time period.

In addition to the brainstorming above look for:

- striking trends

- comparisons/similarities

- overall trends

5. Work out the overall summary. There should be one or two key points that must be mentioned.

6. Plan the structure of answer. (Decide how the data can be grouped into paragraphs).

3.2.   *Sample change over time task*

Cigarette Smoking In Australia

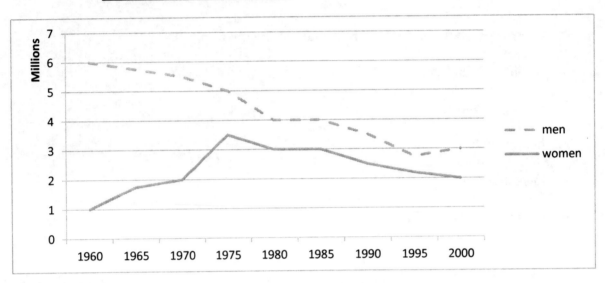

The graph reveals statistics about female and male smokers in Australia between the years 1960 and 2000. Overall, the number of male smokers declined strongly, whereas the total number of female smokers rose slightly. In addition, there are always more male smokers than females throughout the entire period.

The number of men who smoked in 1960 was approximately 6 million but this decreased gradually to 5 million by 1974. Subsequently, it continued to decrease but more steeply to 2.5 million in 2000, which was the lowest point in the entire period surveyed.

In contrast, the popularity of smoking for females fluctuated throughout the period. In 1960 it was very low at only about 1 million. By 1968 this increased by about 100,000 to 1.70 million and increased again but more steeply to reach a peak at 3.2 million in 1977. The number of female smokers then dropped slightly to 2 million by 2000.   [153 words]

Steps to complete the model task

1. Read and underline key vocabulary in the question and write words with the same or related meaning.

2. Check whether the data is about percentages or numbers.

3. Brainstorm key points for the answer, There should be about 10 critical points that should be mentioned for each task)

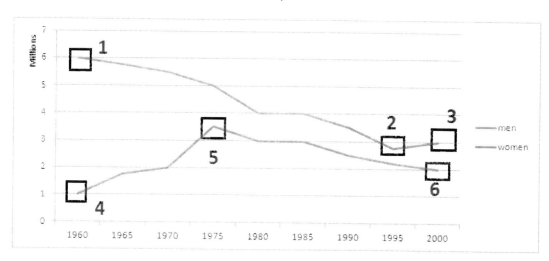

1 = start number for men

2= lowest number for men

3= end number for men

4= start number for women

5= highest number for women

6= end number for women

Below are some additional points worth mentioning.

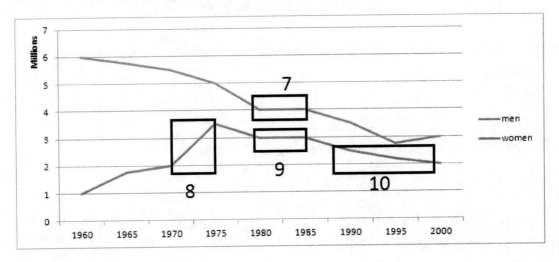

7= plateau for men

8= dramatic increase for women

9= levelled off for women

10= gradual decline for women

5. Work out the overall summary. There should be one or two key points that must be mentioned.

1. Male smokers declined strongly, whereas female smokers rose slightly.

2. There are always more male smokers than females throughout the entire period.

6. Plan the structure of answer. (Establish how can the data be grouped into paragraphs).

Generally speaking it is easier to organise data by the fewest types of categories, so in this case it makes sense to group data by gender and not by time periods. The structure is as follows:

Introduction = rephrase the task introduction + overall summary

men = describe from the starting time period to the end

women = describe from the starting time period to the end

7. Write the task.

The model answer is written above.

4. Process diagram or flow chart

Task Instructions

The IELTS process task is designed to test your ability to compare and contrast information shown in a **process diagram, or flow chart.** You are required to write over 150 words, and the task should be completed in 20 minutes (both part 1 and 2 must be finished in 1 hour).

Requires

1. Articles. Every countable noun needs an article (a, an, the)

2. Passive tense. This is where the sentence starts with the object and the subject of the sentence is often missed out (especially for a man-made process where the subject is often unknown)

3. Sequencers: (first, subsequently, after that, finally)

4. Verbs of process: Verbs are needed to describe putting things in, taking them out, changing one thing into another, or throwing away waste items. (inserted, extracted, transformed into, discarded)

5. 'Non-defining' Relative Clauses are useful for adding extra information about the subject or the object of the sentence

Language for processes

Steps in the process

The first step
The first step in the process is
The first stage in the process is
The process begins with
The process commences with

Subsequent steps
Subsequently,
After this,
The next step is
In the next stage,
In the following stage,
Following this,

The final step
The process finishes with ...
The process concludes with ...
The last step is ...

Describing the location of objects

OBJECT A is…	adjacent to alongside underneath above in the middle of on the right of on the left of	…OBJECT B
OBJECT A is…	between equidistant from	… OBJECT B and OBJECT C

Expressing purpose - why something is done

... in order to ...

... so as to...

As a result,

Eventually,

Consequently,

Passive Form

The passive begins with the object (receiver of the action) and is followed by an auxiliary verb and a main verb in the past participle form. The table below compares the passive to the active tense.

Tense		Verb	
Present Active	Mike	writes	a book.
Present Passive	A book	is written	by Mike.
Past Active	Mike	wrote	a book.
Past Passive	A book	was written	by Mike

Tip!
Passive voice is needed when describing actions where the subject is unknown.

4.1.   *Steps to complete a process diagram task:*

1. Read the question and the process diagram and underline key words.

2. Paraphrase key words where possible.

3. Look for any unlabeled parts of the process and name them if you can.

4. Look for a logical start point for the process.

5. Look for a logical middle point for the process, so that you can separate the data into paragraphs in the body of the report.

6. Look for the logical end point for the process.

7. Number steps in the process to make sure you will not miss out any of the steps when you write your report.

8. Write the report.

9. Proofread the report.

Structuring the task

Introduction

1. Rephrase the question

2. Give an overall summary of the process [= number of steps, number of materials used, amount of equipment used]

Body

Make sure you write about every stage of the process. If there are less than nine steps in the process, I suggest you write a sentence for every step to make sure you can get to the 150 word requirement. If there are more than ten steps you will need to start to combine these steps in your sentences in order to be able to finish on time.

If there is a logical separation point in the process you could divide the steps in the process into two or even more paragraphs.

Note: you should not write a conclusion unless you have less than 150 words. If you need to write a conclusion, you can write a paragraph that rephrases your first paragraph to get to the required 150 word limit.

4.2. Sample process task

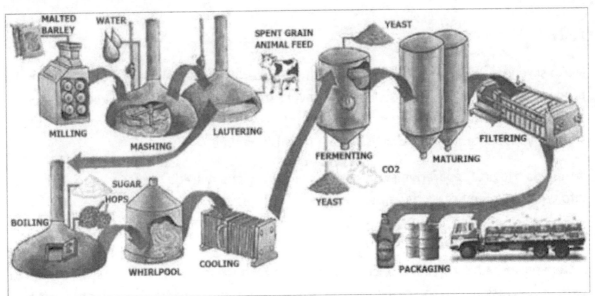

Task taken from: The Complete Guide to Task 1 Writing by Phil Biggerton.

Model answer for a process

The figure illustrates the different steps used to manufacture beer. Overall, there are eleven stages in the process, beginning with the milling of malted barley and ending with packaging the beer.

Looking at first stages of the process, we can see that in order to get liquid from malted barley, it has to be milled, mashed with water and lautered in special tanks. In order to get a pure liquid, the spent grain is taken out and used for feeding of animals. Then, the liquid has to be boiled with sugar and hops and mixed in a whirlpool before cooling.

In the next stages the cooled liquid has to be fermented by adding yeast and carbon dioxide. Then, it goes to storage tanks, in order to be matured. In the second to last stage, the matured beer is transferred to a filter for filtering. Finally, the beer is packed in bottles or barrels or put on trucks for delivery.
[159 words]

Steps to complete the process task

1. Read the question and the process diagram and underline key words. Paraphrase key words where possible; and turn nouns into verbs, and verbs into nouns

   The <u>diagram</u> below <u>shows</u> the <u>various</u> <u>stages</u> <u>involved</u> in the <u>production</u>

   figure   *illustrates*   *different*   *steps*   *used*   *manufacture*

   of <u>beer</u>.

2. Look for any unlabeled parts of the process and name them if you can.

3. Look for a logical start point for the process.
   Step one Adding malted barley [top-left corner of the illustration]

4. Look for a logical middle point for the process, so that you can separate the data into paragraphs in the body of the report
   step eight when the fermenting process begins

5. Look for the logical end point for the process.
   Step 11 packaging

6. Number steps in the process to make sure you will not miss out any of the steps when you write your report.

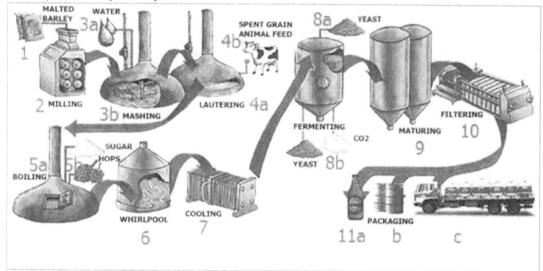

7. Write the report

8. Proofread the report

45

5. Map or floor plan

Task Instructions

The IELTS map or floor plan task is designed to test your ability to compare and contrast information shown in a **map** or **floor plan** of a building. You are required to write over 150 words, and the task should be completed in 20 minutes (both part 1 and 2 must be finished in 1 hour).

Requires

1. Articles: Every countable noun needs an article (a, an, the).

2. Passive tense: This is where the sentence starts with the object and the subject of the sentence is often missed out (especially for developments where the subject is often unknown, for example, "a building was constructed").
    [Note this is explained in the previous section on process tasks.]

3. Language to describe locations (north, south....adjacent to, across from).

4. Verbs of change: Verbs are needed to describe things being added, removed, or changed (constructed, demolished, transformed).

5. 'Non-defining' Relative Clauses are useful for adding extra information about the subject or the object of the sentence.

> *Tip!*
> **If you get a map or floor plan task always look to see if there is a compass on it so that you can use it to describe the location of objects.**

Language to describe locations

Compass points

You can use the table below to describe the points on the compass.

Note the following rules about capitalisation:

1. Don't capitalise points of a compass when describing a general location or direction. For example: *In the north of the map is a house.*

2. Capitalise for names. For example: *The house is in North America.*

northwest	north	northeast
west		east
southwest	south	southeast

Describing location if there is no compass or to rephrase compass points

Every real test paper I have seen has had a compass on it. If you ever get one that doesn't or if you want to show your ability to rephrase you can use the expressions below. For example: *In the top left of the map is a house.*

top-left	top	top-right
left		right
bottom-left	bottom	bottom-right

Describing locations

In the central part of the map...

In front of [the house]...

Behind...

Next to...

Adjacent to...

Describe objects which are nearby:

Next to...

Within easy reach of a...

It is not far from...

Use comparison and contrast words.

Twice as big as...

Not as big as...

Half the size of...

It is smaller/ bigger than...

There are more/less ...than ...

Closer to...

Further away from...

5.1.   Planning a map task

1. Read the question and the map/floor plan and underline key words.

2. Paraphrase keywords that are given in the question where possible.

3. Look for a compass so that you can know whether you can use it for describing locations.

4. Brainstorm key points for the answer. There should be about 10 critical points that should be mentioned for each task.

5. Work out the overall summary. There should be one or two key points that must be mentioned.

6. Plan the structure of answer (how can the data be grouped).

7. Write the task.

8. Proofread the task.

5.2.   Single map task

A task where you are only given one map usually requires you to choose between two proposed locations. Past test papers have included things like where to build a new shopping centre, supermarket, and train station. In order to complete this task you should compare the two proposed sites in terms of the feature of their surrounding areas. You may also compare the actual sizes of each of the sites. Sometimes each site will be the same size but sometimes there may be a difference in the size of buildings, and even other aspects such as car parks.

> *Tip!*
> **Single map tasks are used to test your ability to compare two locations on a map.**

Structuring a single map task

When you get a task with two proposed sites on a map you can use the structure below.

Introduction

1. Rephrase the task introduction.

2. Give an overall summary of the differences between the two locations on the map. Essentially you need to point out what is the key difference between the two locations. The main differences are likely to be the relative size of each of the sites and their proximity to amenities such as roads, transportation networks or buildings such as hospitals and recreational facilities. If you are given a floor plan the most likely changes are aspects such as the proximity to entry ways, or facilities such as coffee making machines or photocopiers.

Body

As with other tasks you should always look for a logical way to separate the data into paragraphs in the body. For this type of task it is very easy to separate data. You can have a paragraph for each of the sites. When describing each site you can first discuss the advantages of the site and then possibly the disadvantages. It may not always be appropriate to discuss the disadvantages because sometimes the disadvantages of one site are the advantages for the other.

The other important thing about writing the body of this type of task is to pick a logical starting point to begin your description and then state clearly where this is located on the map. Remember that your report should always make sense without the examiner looking at the map. After you have just described the location of the first feature you can then move on to discuss other features in relation to that first feature. Note that for Western logic it is usual to describe things from left to right [which on the map is going to be west to east, and from north to south]. The worst way to write the body paragraphs is to just jump around all different locations of the map at random.

Note: you should not write a conclusion unless you have less than 150 words. For the conclusion you can write a paragraph that rephrases your first paragraph to get to the required 150 word limit.

5.3.   Sample task for a single map

You should spend about 20 minutes on this task.

The map below shows two different proposed locations for a camping ground.

Summarise the information by selecting and reporting the main features, and make comparisons where relevant.

Write at least 150 words.

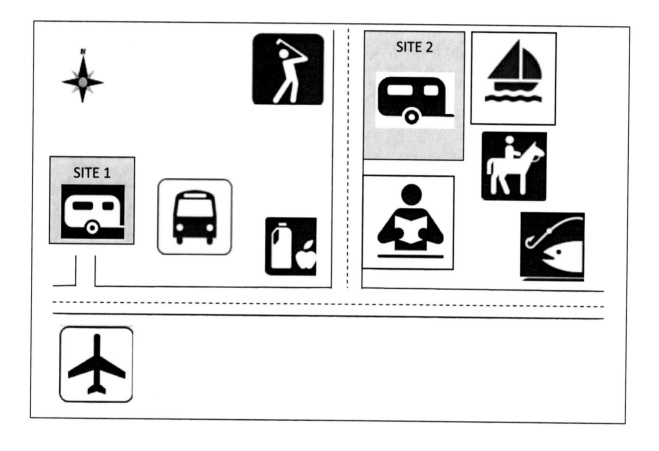

Model answer

The picture illustrates two potential positions for camping sites. Overall, site one is smaller and located nearer to amenities, while site two is larger and closer to recreational activities.

Site 1 is located on the west side of the map and it is the smaller of the two sites. The main advantage of this site is its proximity to transportation facilities. It is across the road from the airport and has a bus stop next to it. In addition there is a grocery store down the road to the east.

Turning to site 2, which is located in the north-east of the map, it is a much larger site. Moreover it is located very close to many entertainment activities. To the east campers can go boating or horse riding. South of the site there is a library and a place to go fishing. As well as this across the road to the west there is a golf course.

[157 words]

Steps to complete the model task

1. Read the task introduction for the map and underline and rephrase key words.

   The <u>map</u> below <u>shows</u> <u>two</u> <u>different</u> <u>proposed</u> <u>locations</u> for a <u>camping ground</u>.

   picture   illustrates   potential   positions   camping   sites

2. Look for a compass so that you can know whether you can use it for describing locations.
   yes there is a compass! [In the top left corner]

3. Look for a dividing feature of the body of the report.
   each of the two sites will be a body paragraph

4. Look for any unlabeled parts of the map and name them if you can.

   bus stop, grocery store, library, place for boating, horse riding, fishing

5. Number key points of the map to make sure you will not miss out any of these features

   when you write your report.

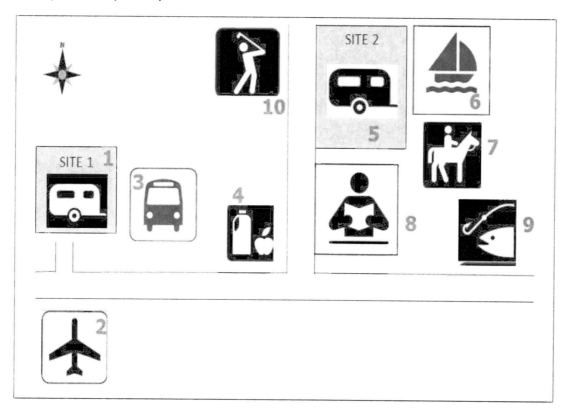

6. Work out the overall summary.

   Site 1 is smaller and it is closer to transportation facilities

   Site 2 is larger and it is closer to entertainment facilities

7. Plan the structure of answer (how can the data be grouped).

   Introduction

   site 1

   site 2

8. Write the report.

9. Proofread the report.

Model report with the comparative words underlined

The picture illustrates two potential positions for camping sites. Overall, site one is <u>smaller</u> and located <u>nearer</u> to amenities, while site two is <u>larger</u> and <u>closer</u> to recreational activities.

Site 1 is located on the west side of the map and it is the smaller of the two sites. The main advantage of this site is its close proximity to transportation facilities. It is across the road from the airport and has a bus stop next to it. In addition, there is a grocery store down the road to the east.

Turning to site 2, which is located in the north-east of the map, it is a <u>much larger</u> site. Moreover it is located <u>very close</u> to many entertainment activities. To the east campers can go boating or horse riding. South of the site there is a library and a place to go fishing. As well as this across the road to the west there is a golf course.

Model report with the location words underlined

The picture illustrates two potential positions for camping sites. Overall, site one is smaller and located nearer to amenities, while site two is larger and closer to recreational activities.

Site 1 is <u>located on the west</u> of the map and it is the smaller of the two sites. The main advantage of this site is its proximity to transportation facilities. It is <u>across the road from</u> the airport and has a bus stop <u>next to it</u>. In addition, there is a grocery store <u>down the road to the east</u>.

Turning to site 2, which is <u>located in the north-east</u> of the map, it is a much larger site. Moreover it is <u>located very close to</u> many entertainment activities. <u>To the east</u> campers can go boating or horse riding. <u>South of the site</u> there is a library and a place to go fishing. As well as this across the road to the west there is a golf course.

5.4.   Double map task

When you are given two maps the key point is to compare these maps and highlight the main changes that have occurred. These are likely to be things being added, removed or being turned into different things.

Describing changes using past passive tense

Added	was constructed was built was erected
Removed	were cut down was replaced
Changed	was converted was turned into was transformed was replaced with was changed into
Stayed the same	remained

> **Tip!**
> Tasks with two maps are used to test your ability to identify changes that have occurred between these two maps.

Structuring a double map task

When you get a task with two or more maps you can use the structure below.

Introduction

1. Rephrase the task introduction.

2. Give an overall summary of the differences between the maps. Essentially you need to point out what is the key difference. For maps of the town it is usually from a small undeveloped place into a much larger more developed place. The more developed place is often a tourist centre or has a much better transportation network. For a floor plan the most likely changes are for a larger building and a smaller outdoor area; or, a change in the number of rooms.

Body

As with other tasks you should always look for a logical way to separate the data into paragraphs in the body. There are two ways to do this. The first is to write a paragraph about each map. In this case the first paragraph will describe the most notable features of the first map. The second paragraph will describe the changes that have occurred, which are likely to be things being removed added or changed.

The second way to structure the body is to look for a dividing feature in the map like a river or road in the middle of it. Then each of the body paragraphs describes each of the sides. Even if you follow the previous structure of writing a body paragraph about each map, it is still a good idea to look for a dividing feature and structure each of these paragraphs according to that dividing feature.

The other important thing about writing the body of this type of task is to pick a logical starting point to begin your description and then state clearly where this is located on the map. Remember that your report should always make sense without the examiner looking at the map. After you have just described the location of the first feature you can then move on to discuss other features in relation to that first feature. Note that for Western logic it is usual to describe things from left to right [which on the map is going to be west to east, and from north to south]. The worst way to write the body paragraphs is to just jump around all different locations of the map at random.

Note: you should not write a conclusion unless you have less than 150 words. For the conclusion you can write a paragraph that rephrases your first paragraph to get to the required 150 word limit.

5.5.   Sample of a double map task

The maps below show how the town of Harborne changes from 1936 to 2007. Summarise the information by selecting and reporting the main features, and make comparisons where relevant.

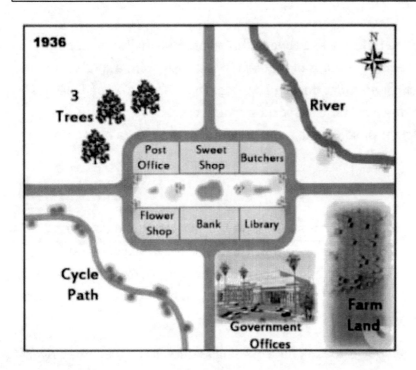

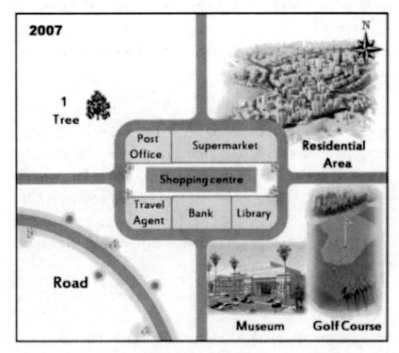

Task taken from: The Complete Guide to Task 1 Writing by Phil Biggerton.

Model answer for a map

The illustrations reveal changes that occurred in the township of Harborne from 1936 to 2007. Overall, the town became a much larger residential area with more shops.

Many changes occurred west of the city. In the north-west most of the trees were cut down, and in the south-west the bicycle track was converted into a roadway. In the centre of the city, the post office, bank, and library remained. However, in the northern section the candy store and butchers shop were converted into a grocery store. A shopping centre was constructed in the centre of the downtown replacing most of the open space there. In the southern part the flower shop became a travel agent.

North-east of the downtown area the river was turned into a lake and a large residential area was built on its shores with lots of high-rise apartments. Meanwhile, in the south-east the government offices were transformed into a museum and the farmland became a golf course.

[160 words]

Steps to complete the model task

1. Read the task introduction for the map and rephrase key words.

   Paraphrase key words where possible.

   The <u>maps</u> below <u>show</u> how the <u>town</u> of Harborne <u>changes</u> from 1936 to 2007.

   illustrations   reveal   township   changes that occurred

2. Look for a compass so that you can know whether you can use it for describing locations - *yes there is a compass*!

3. Look for a dividing feature in the centre of the map.
   the downtown area

4. Look for any unlabeled parts of the map and name them if you can.
   high-rise apartments [in the north-east]

5. Look for a logical start point for describing the map.
   north-west of the downtown area seems like a good starting point

6. Look for a logical middle point for the map, so that you can separate the data into paragraphs in the body of the report.
   the downtown area

7. Number key points of the map to make sure you will not miss out any of these features when you write your report.

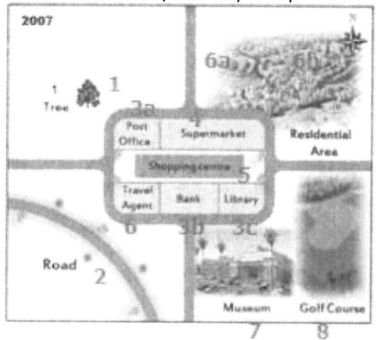

8. Plan the structure of answer (how can the data be grouped)

Introduction

West and downtown area

East area

9. Write the report

10. Proofread the report

Verbs used to describe changes are underlined below

The illustrations reveal changes that occurred in the township of Harborne from 1936 to 2007. Overall, the town became a <u>much larger residential area</u> with <u>more shops</u>.

Many changes occurred west of the city. In the north-west most of the trees <u>were cut down</u>, and in the south-west the bicycle track <u>was converted</u> into a roadway. In the centre of the city, the post office, bank, and library <u>remained</u>. However in the northern section the candy store and butchers shop <u>were converted</u> into a supermarket. A shopping centre <u>was constructed</u> in the centre of the downtown replacing most of the open space there. In the southern part the flower shop became a travel agent.

North-east of the downtown area the river <u>was turned into</u> a lake and a large residential area <u>was built</u> on its shores with lots of high-rise apartments. Meanwhile, in the south-east the government offices <u>were transformed</u> into a museum and the farmland became a golf course.

Exercise 3: Verbs describing change

All the verbs used to describe the changes made are underlined above try to categorise these according to the function of these verbs in the table below. You can check your answers at the back of the book.

Added	1
	2
Removed	3
Changed	4
	5
	6
Stayed the same	7

5.6.   Sample task for a floor plan

The floor plans below show the changes that were made to a house over a six-month period.

Before — Meals, Kitchen, Living, Bath, Bedroom, ROBE, Bedroom, Entry, ROBE, Verandah

After — Kitch., Meals, Living, Bath, Bed, Entry, Bed

Model answer for a floor plan

The illustrations reveal the alterations that occurred at a residential building. Overall, the main difference is that the renovated building has one less internal wall.

Looking at the point of entry to the house in the middle, there is no longer a porch in the updated house. In addition, on the left side of the house the wall has been removed between the sitting room and kitchen to make one large living space, with a dining table placed in the middle. The cooking area has been moved to the right-hand wall of the kitchen, and there is no longer an area for eating in the rear of the kitchen.

Turning to the right-hand side of the house, in the rear the bathroom has been modified by moving the toilets to the middle of the room and replacing the bathtub with a shower. The wardrobes have been removed from both bedrooms. In addition, the window has been removed from the rear bedroom, while the front bedroom has a smaller window.

[169]

Steps to complete the model task

1. Read the task introduction for the map and rephrase key words.

    The floor plans below show the changes that were made to a house.

    illustrations reveal alterations occurred residential building

2. Look for a compass so that you can know whether you can use it for describing locations. *-no compass*

3. Look for a dividing feature in the centre of the map.
    the hallway and entrance

4. Look for any unlabeled parts of the map and name them if you can.
    windows; bathtub [before] shower [after; dining table [after]

5. Look for a logical start point for describing the map.
    The veranda and entry seems like a good starting point.

6. Look for a logical middle point for the map, so that you can separate the data into paragraphs in the body of the report.
    the downtown area

> *Tip!*
> **With a floor plan it can be difficult to find a logical start point. The key point is to pick a location and then make sure it is clear to the reader where this is**

7. Number key points of the map to make sure you will not miss out any of these features when you write your report.

8. Plan the structure of answer. (how can the data be grouped)

Introduction

West and downtown area

East area

9. Write the report.

10. Proofread the report.

6. Future period tasks

Sometimes in the exam you are given date that concerns a future time period. In this case, the future data is a prediction or forecast, and you must make this clear when writing your report. You cannot state it in the present tense as a fact. You must make it clear to the examiner that this information is only a forecast. If you fail to do this you are making a factual error and your score for task achievement will be lowered.

Language for expressing a prediction

Words to express a prediction: predicted, expected, forecasted, anticipated

Future tense: will, is going to

It is <u>predicted</u> that the use of solar energy <u>will</u> rise.

It is <u>anticipated</u> that the use of solar energy <u>is going to</u> rise.

Note about the following task

The report is produced in 2010 so we can establish that all data before this point has actually occurred and everything after this date is a projection.

6.1. Sample future task

You should spend about 20 minutes on this task

The graph below gives information from a report in 2010 about the use of energy in Australia since 1980 with projections until 2030.

Summarize the information by selecting and reporting the main features, and make comparisons where relevant.

Write at least 150 words

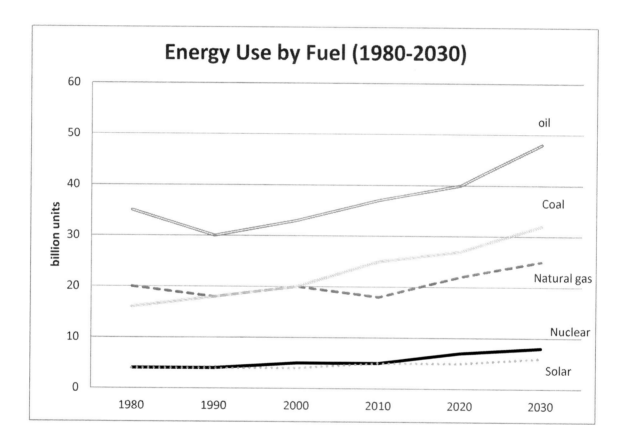

> *Tip!*
> **When describing data about the future it is essential you
> make it clear that the data is only a prediction.**

Model answer

Given is a line graph, which displays energy consumption in Australia from 1980 to 2030; the energy is divided into different categories according to fuel sources. Overall, it can be seen that there is an upward trend for all types of energy except during the period from 1980 to 2010, and this trend is predicted to continue up to and including 2030.

In 1980, 35 billion units of oil were used to generate energy. Fluctuations in the first 15 years notwithstanding, the units of consumption experienced a steady growth from 1995 onwards, and projections show the usage will hit about 48 billion by 2030. Even though coal starts the graph much lower at 16 billion units and natural gas at 20 billion units, they are both expected to consistently climb to end at 32 billion and 25 billion units, respectively, with the usage of coal now ahead by approximately 7 billion units.

Standing at 4 billion units in 1980, nuclear and solar energy underwent a marginal increase in their consumption units, and are expected to reach 8 billion and 6 billion units, respectively, in 2030, according to estimates.

[189 words]

Model answer with the future predictions underlined

Given is a line graph, which displays energy consumption in Australia from 1980 to 2030; the energy is divided into different categories according to fuel sources. Overall, it can be seen that there is an upward trend for all types of energy during the period from 1980 to 2010, and this trend is <u>predicted to continue</u> up to and including 2030.

In 1980, 35 billion units of oil were used to generate energy. Fluctuations in the first 15 years notwithstanding, the units of consumption experienced a steady growth from 1995 onwards, and <u>projections show the usage will hit</u> about 48 billion by 2030. Even though coal starts the graph much lower at 16 billion units and natural gas at 20 billion units, they <u>are both expected to consistently climb</u> to end at 32 billion and 25 billion units, respectively, with the usage of coal now ahead by approximately 7 billion units.

Standing at 4 billion units in 1980, nuclear and solar energy underwent a marginal increase in their consumption units, and <u>are expected to reach</u> 8 billion and 6 billion units, respectively, in 2030, <u>according to estimates</u>.

7. Vocabulary

General trend:

From the data it is evident that the majority of...

With a cursory glance, it can clearly be seen from the information provided that...

The most striking feature of the chart is that...

The most noticeable characteristic of the chart is that...

Linking Phrases:

Initially,

According to the data collected...

Most noteworthy, is the fact that...

More specifically, from the point of view of...

In direct contrast, ...

In stark contrast, ...

However,...

Table:

Tabular numeric data is presented that shows...

The rows show information about...

The columns show data concerning...

Pie chart:

The pie chart/graph reveals data concerning ...

The largest sector of the graph is for...

Bar graph:

The bar chart/graph reveals...

Each bar represents...

Line chart:

This line chart/graph) displays information as a series of data points connected by straight line segments.

The vertical axis represents...

The horizontal axis shows...

Map

Given is a map of... illustrating ... in relation to ... as well as ....

As shown in the figure...

Language of approximation

Just under; well under; just over; well over

Roughly; nearly; approximately; around; about

Language for similar information

Similarly,...

Likewise,...

At the same rate as,...

By the same token,...

Language for different information

differ from; dissimilarly; unlike; different from

Language for increases

Double/twofold/ increased two times

Triple/ treble/ threefold/ increased three times

Quadruple/ four times

Sixfold

Language for decreases

A half/ half; one third/ by a third; one fourth/ quarter; one-fifth; one-tenth

Language to describe Time

over the period

during the period in question

during the first period

prior to

a decade earlier in the subsequent decade

from 1990 onwards

in the latter half of a year

in the last quarter

8. Sentence structures

In order to score well for grammar, it is important to show a range of sentence types. This can easily be achieved by using different structures for your sentences. Different structures can be created by changing the order of information and the placement of data in the sentence.

S + I + D

Subject   **Importance**   **Data**

Example   Subject: Australia

Importance: the biggest producer of steel

Data: 70 billion tonnes per year

S + I + D

Australia is the biggest producer of steel at 70 billion tonnes tons per year.

D + I + S

At 70 million tons per year, the biggest producer of steel in the world is Australia.

I + D + S

The biggest producer of steel in the world, at 70 million tons of steel per year, is Australia.

I + S + D

The biggest producer of steel in the world is Australia at 70 million tons per year.

S + D + I

Australia, at 70 million tons per year, is the biggest producer of steel in the world.

D + S + I

At 70 million tons per year, Australia is the biggest producer of steel in the world.

Example using more than one structure:

It is interesting to note that at 70 million tons of steel per year, Australia is the biggest producer in the world followed by Canada with the second largest amount of steel production at 65 million tons.

Tip!
Use a wide range of sentence structures to increase your score for grammar

9. Answers

Exercise 1: Comparatives and Superlatives

	comparative	superlative
1. accurate	more accurate	most accurate
2. certain	more certain	most certain
3. pretty	prettier	prettiest
4. cool	cooler	coolest
5. correct	more correct	most correct
6. dangerous	more dangerous	most dangerous
7. easy	easier	easiest
8. modern	more modern	most modern
9. funny	funnier	funniest
10. new	newer	newest
11. possible	more possible	most possible
12. probable	more probable	most probable
13. up-to-date	more up-to-date	most up-to-date

Exercise 2: Language with numbers and percentages

1. The number/~~amount~~ of cars was over 1,000.

2. The rate/ ~~number~~ of electricity usage was 15 per cent.

3. The ~~amount~~ /percentage of power was 15%

4. The number/~~amount~~ of trains was 100.

5. The ~~number~~ /proportion of lamb consumed increased by 15 percent.

6. The percentage/~~amount~~ of lamb (15%) and chicken (16%) were about the same.

7. The ~~number~~/amount of beer consumed was 100 litres.

8. The proportion/ ~~amount~~ of water usage and power usage were 15% and 16%, respectively.

9. The number/ ~~percentage~~ of apples was 10 on Fridays.

10. The ~~number~~/amount of oil produced was 100 litres.

Exercise 3: Verbs describing change

Added	1	was constructed
	2	was built
Removed	3	were cut down
Changed	4	was converted
	5	was turned into
	6	were transformed
Stayed the same	7	remained

SPECIAL OFFER

Thank you for purchasing my book and taking the time to read it. I hope that it will be beneficial and help you to achieve the score you need in the IELTS writing exam.

As a sign of appreciation I would like to offer you a free correction of your task 1 report using my editing and correction services. In order to take advantage of this offer, please send me an e-mail of your letter and the invoice number for purchasing this book. My e-mail address is: mike@IELTSanswers.com

I believe it is extremely beneficial to have an experienced person read your essays and give you feedback on how to improve them. This can avoid many of the typical errors that occur on test day and help you to maximise your score.

CPSIA information can be obtained at www.ICGtesting.com
Printed in the USA
LVOW09s2239310715

448467LV00013B/295/P